MUR MUR ATI ON

BLAKE AUDEN

central
avenue
PUBLISHING

2021

Published by Central Avenue Publishing, an imprint of Central Avenue Marketing Ltd.
www.centralavenuepublishing.com

MURMURATION

Trade Paper: 978-1-77168-252-7
Epub: 978-1-77168-253-4
Mobi: 978-1-77168-254-1

Published in Canada
Printed in United States of America

1. POETRY / Subjects & Themes - Love   2. Poetry / Grief

10 9 8 7 6 5 4 3 2 1

for the city i call home.

the sea's exhale breaks around my feet
and for a moment we are both   still.
above the waves, a mass of starlings
twists and collapses in on itself
before bursting out in an explosion of tiny bones.

i watch the birds beyond the iron carrion
and by now the water has reached my knees.
i look down and wonder
if any amount of salt could purge
the monsters from my blood.

ONE

i held my fingers
against your hallowed skin
and i wanted to break you open,
but not in the way i did.

i wanted to kneel
at the altar of your ribs,
but i didn't want
to take them with me.

i can't keep holding
sacrament on my tongue
when longing is already
too close to prayer,

when i have no holy places
left to shelter.

it's no good
waiting for flowers
if all you lay
in the earth
is bone

i will take it all back
if you want me to.
all the soft words
and late-night promises.

i can pretend
my tongue doesn't still find
the shape of your name,
and leave you to forget
what we were.

i swear, i won't write
another word
if it means
you can be happy.

i have broken bones
that once belonged to you,
which is to say
i am your son.

but the word *mother*
is lost in my mouth,

because the edges are whetted with grief
and i don't know how to speak it
with the gratitude
it deserves.

because i can't give back
the borrowed blood

i lost in places
i never should have been.
because i speak of ambition
like this was never enough,

and the words *thank you*
don't fall from my mouth

as often as they should.
because you are the world
and i am a river,
and i can't carry

everything you are when words
are the only current i have.

THERE

IS

A

CRUEL

IRONY

IN

BEING

A

WRITER

WHO

IS

TERRIFIED

OF

ENDINGS

i surround
myself
with trees
     in the hope
     i might become
a growing thing, too.

can you tell us about yourself?
and suddenly, i've forgotten why i'm here.

nobody wants an honest answer
to that question anyway.

all the plants i own are plastic, because
i've never known how to stop anything good from dying, or

i hate everyone in this room
for assuming their grief is the same as mine.

i leave, as usual, and within minutes
i'm back at the sea,

time lost to the churning tide-breaths
and the fevered call of the gulls,

and i understand it, i think:

in some way or another,
every cry is one of hunger.

i remember
so little
of the day we met.

i'm sure
you said something
                beautiful,

but all i could hear
was the sound
of my heartbeat,

a broken organ
repeating,
i swear to god, that's her.

what am i
if not
this daily
surrender?

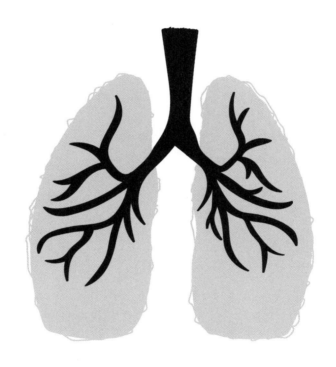

you held me
the way lungs
hold our breath.

i guess the exhale
was inevitable.

i don't know
what healing
is meant
to look like,
but washing
the smell of you
from my hoodie
feels like
a good place
to start.

YOU WOULD
LOOK AT ME
WITH THOSE
SALTWATER
     EYES
AND I WOULD
SEE NOTHING
BUT A REFLECTION
    OF HOME

of all
the things
i have
survived
it breaks
my heart
that you
had to be
one
        of
  them

the morning is copper
and cursed, and i don't
know how to hold it softly enough
to keep it from breaking.

i am too heavy
for what is left,
and i can see falling
in the autumn of your eyes.

you talk in echoes,
and i can only pull the ashes
of summer through the ruin
in my throat.

this is the last
of the things we shared.
the last of the sun-brushed
horizons to meet us.

maybe
you were right.

maybe
i am scared
of forever.

maybe
i can't love something
that isn't
a dying thing, too.

[The thunder sounds like the
collapse of a city in the distance,
and all I can think about is how
your name has become a rotten
tooth in my mouth, about how
I'm still not brave enough
to take pliers to my jaw.
When you're young and they
tell you that love is immortal,
this is what they mean:
not that it's timeless; they mean
it's undying. They mean it clings
to your rib cage with clawed hands,
that the definition of an ending
is subjective, elastic. They mean that
eventually, it will teach you how
a man can crumble under the weight
of a name.]

i want you to know
that i see it, and that i think
we are a ground knuckle.

we are not
the people we once were.

our bodies stridulate
against each other, and it sounds
like something is dying,

like there is a monster
inside us both.

maybe this is what love
really is: a light touch
between snapping beasts,

an orchid forcing its way
through concrete.

you scratch
        survivor
into my skin

and tell me
we're the same.

but to survive
is to drag yourself
from the water

and forget what it is
to swallow salt.

i am living,
but have survived
        nothing.

i am a bruised body,
trying to remember

how to swim.

love is not
all that different to loss

if you look at them
in shallow light

and what i know
of both

i know of the contours
of your skin

this place
wields silence
like a closed fist.

by which i mean,
i miss the sound
of your laugh.

i'll sit here
amongst the judas trees
and watch the birds
at their evening work.

i want you to know
that i'm okay,
                   really.

i still love you,
but i swear i think of you
with a smile,

and the word *goodbye*
is no longer carrion
in my throat.

maybe healing
is just a matter
of distance,

between me
and her smile,

between the deer
and the bullet.

in the end
i am
a paper tiger,

a man
who writes
of love

when he spends
his days
afraid of it.

i'm awake because i picked a hole
in my skin as i slept.
and this isn't a metaphor,
  although maybe it should be.

the sheets are slick with blood
that won't stop running,
so eager to leave before it's wasted.

this has been a tough year,
and now they tell me
not to leave the house.

the tissue's white gives way
to august red, and i'm sure, now.
i wouldn't leave this place
  if it burst into flames.

i am no longer
the soft thing i was.

i am more bone
than embrace,

more the riverbed
than the water.

[I don't remember becoming so sharp,
a body of thistle and calcified edges.
You didn't do this to me, but the boy
you left was softer, someone you could
love without the cutting of skin.
I think the body learns how to protect
itself, to harden and coil. I think the body
learns to offer thorns in the hope of
saving what's left of the flower.
I think this is what it means to be a
hunted thing.]

to love something
is to accept its ability
to hurt you,

to allow something
to grow and bloom
in your chest

knowing you will
carry it
long after it decays.

your name
is the softest word
i have
for suffocation.
the gentlest way
i know
to drown.

I THINK
ALL OF THIS
IS JUST A WAY
TO GET YOU
OUT OF ME

the truth is
this body
has withstood more

than i ever thought it could.

the truth is
i'm stronger
than i want to be.

these bones

      will heal

  and yet

           remember nothing

    of breaking

i watch the wren,
frantic
and searching
in the lifeless green,

and i can feel it
in the grinding
crater
of my throat:

we all suffer
the weight
of longing;
we are all cursed

with the hunger
of want.

maybe we are designed
to break,

to be taught how much
we can take
and still endure.

maybe this is how
the future survives the past.

it was all i could do
to find space to breathe
between the words,

not to pull out my ribs
to show you i could still
make room in my chest.

[Sometimes, the words grow thorns
of their own. Sometimes they catch
and tear and no amount of clawing
can pull them from my neck.
When you told me I was impossible
to love, I said nothing, because it was all
I could do to find space to breathe
between the words—not to pull out
my ribs to show you I could still make
room in my chest. You once told me I was
a broken boy, in love with the pieces.
That there was no room for you amongst
the bees in my head. I didn't disagree
with you. Instead, I watched you leave,
knowing you'd be happier without me.
Maybe letting you go was the only way
I could prove it to you: I could love you
more than the monsters that make me
who I am.]

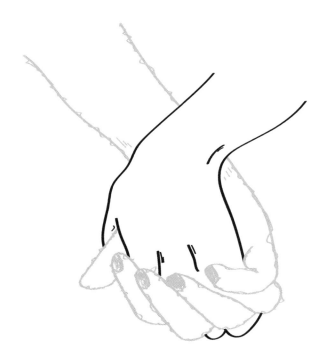

i'm not sure you exist anymore.

i've been putting you back together
from fragments of memories,
            moments,
                torn photographs.

the version of you
i hold in my head
isn't real

and i'm in love
with the ghosts of your hands
in mine.

this emptiness
has a weight to it,

like every
taken breath

draws nothing
but gravity

into my lungs.

hope
lives here,
still.

but she is
a fragile
thing,

a trembled
bird
                    resting

in these
lead-heavy
hands.

i bought you flowers
and you planted them
in the garden.

this way they will live forever.

i message to say
you're the only person i know
that can't bear

to let anything die.

what i don't tell you
is that you're always
fracturing soil

just so you can fill the hole.

that i think you're desperate
to see something root.

something grow.
        something stay.

i've been watching
the swallows
gather outside my window.

they're ready
to leave again,
and it makes me think of you.

(some beating hearts
seem to know
exactly where they're meant to be.)

TWO

you would say
i love you
like it was
a suicide note,

like it was
the last bloom
of the dahlias
before the grip
of winter.

[I've been thinking recently about how things were for you, and how hard it must have been to love someone who can only exist in pieces. I know your childhood was tough. I know the things you went through left scars on your body, and I think they left their mark on your heart, too. The truth is I'm not sure you know how to let someone love you without expecting them to leave. You would tell me that you loved me, and some days it sounded like goodbye. I guess what I'm trying to say is I understand, and there's nothing for me to forgive.]

i swear, i'm fine.

by which i mean
i'm eating enough
to keep me alive.

i was born with rivers
in my mouth

and they don't
have the mercy
to drown me.

SOME DAYS
POETRY IS
THE STITCHES

OTHER DAYS
IT'S THE WOUND

i know it would be better
to let go, move on.

but i know this in the same way
the wood knows it's best
to resist the fire.

maybe we don't get to choose
how long we burn.

maybe we don't get to choose
what the flames leave behind.

you can build an altar from rib,
let your knees kiss the pavement
and call it worship.

because even depression
can be a god
if you're afraid enough of it.

the world
is ending

and i'm still
thinking

about you.

the truth is,
worlds end

every day,

and digging soil
isn't the only

way
to make

a grave.

i'm sorry for a lot of things
but mostly for the wound i became.

for convincing you that love
didn't have to hurt

and then carving it
into your bones.

i have always been
a godless thing.

which is to say,
he wants nothing more
to do with me.

i'm sure i grew
from the riverbed

and he hung broken
around my neck
like an epithet.

some days
i speak your name
and taste seawater,
and this can't be
how it's supposed
to feel.

all the words
weigh nothing
until they leave
your mouth

[I've been thinking about the weight
of things recently. About how love is so
light when you're holding it, yet somehow
heavy when it's gone. I've also been
thinking about the words, about how some
are harder to carry, but they all weigh
nothing until they leave your mouth.
I guess these are the things poets think
about. The poetry was light, too, or at least
it was when I was next to you. The words
just grew from my mouth and I would
find them all over your skin. They don't
grow like that anymore; these days I need
to pull them like an anchor from my chest.
Today, everything is heavier than it used
to be. Everything is sharp enough to break
the skin.]

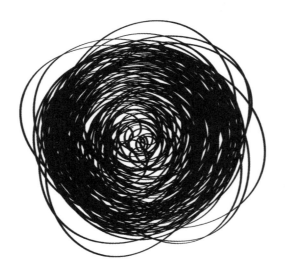

you place
hope
in my palms

knowing
i can't hold
something

so fragile
in these
hurricane hands

of course
i still miss you.

it's the nature
of every dying thing

to do all it can
to stay.

days like this,

i bare my chest to the sky
and still it feels
like the light can't find me,

like everything
but the darkness
has forgotten my name.

IT

WAS

ALWAYS

YOU.

YOU,

WHO FELT

LIKE WATER

WHEN MY

WHOLE BODY

WAS A

FLAME.

WHAT SOFT TORTURE
TO LOVE THAT
WHICH YOU
CANNOT HOLD

i would tell you
how it feels to miss you
the way other people
draw breath,

but there are
some words that can
only be spoken
in darkness,

can only be
brought to life
in places where the light
can't touch them.

i'm still holding on
far tighter
than i should be

because i never learned
that to squeeze
is to risk suffocation,

that under
enough pressure,
everything will break.

the truth is
you fell in love
with the words
and not
the broken hands
that wrote them

[If I'm honest, I think you were in love
with the idea of being with a poet.
You wanted the words, but not the process.
You loved the things I wrote for you, but the
reality of being with someone broken
enough to write them was too much. I think
you wanted the artist, not the tortured, and
I don't blame you. I don't know how you
managed to hold the edges of me for so long,
how you were able to grip the pieces even
when they cut into your hands. I still don't
know how you were ever brave enough to
love me.]

some days
it feels like the shadows

around me
are broken only

by the light
of dead things.

       like i am surrounded
       by ghosts.

the air
thick with silence
as the sheets cling
to my skin
like a missing lover.

your dying hands
now replaced
with my own,
this body spent
and trembling.

i am surrendered
to the memory
and broken, now

         yearning

for an abyss.

instead, the month breaks softly,
falling back into the lulling fog.

the view beyond the oak
is lost to a turning white,

and i wonder if mine
is the only heartbeat left.

if you want honesty
then here it is:

some days i want
to step into the rain,

set myself on fire and see
which of the elements wins out.

but this is just a moment,
a single stone

on a pebble beach.
if you like,

we can fill our pockets
with moments

and walk ourselves
into the sea.

and the girl
(everything
      and gone)

still touches me
with those
cracking fingers

somewhere
other
than here,

the memory
like a handful
of water.

don't let me in.

this heart has grown
into a feral thing,

all wide eyes
and clicking jaw.

the edges of me
are tapered, ossified,

not something
you can hold.

not something you should love.

maybe grief
is a mountain

that needs
to be climbed.

maybe the path
toward healing

is always uphill,
always steep.

but you don't
have to scale it

alone.

these days
my hands
are shifting,
    trembling things.

i am more
earthquake
than anything else.

i carve
forgiveness
from my collarbone
and lay it
gently at my feet.
one day,
i might just
be able
to take it.

every time
i feel myself breaking,

i look to the birds
and i'm reminded

that fragility
can still be beautiful.

LETTING YOU
   WALK AWAY
WAS THE LAST
WAY I KNEW
   HOW TO LOVE YOU

some days are just a search
for new ways to be quiet,

to somehow make myself
                    smaller.

this mouth is sewn shut
with the smile you taught me.

see, it's all just sleight of hand
and (like any good trick)

nobody really wants to know
          how it's done.

breathless
amongst the
dew-wrapped blades,
because it all
feels easier to hold
out here.

above me,
thick branches
accommodate the wind,
their slow
creaking
echoing my own.

the panic
lessens
like a dying applause
and i stay
            still
waiting to be found.

i am
a child of autumn,

at home amongst things

that know only
of falling.

[I have always found comfort in the natural world, the way the trees speak of growth, the birds of survival. But I feel the most resonance in the slow death of autumn, in the way the branches lose themselves until they reveal only bone. There is something vulnerable about their shedding: the revelation of their true selves. I find inspiration in this vulnerability, in their ability to remain strong after such loss. To grow again, in time.]

this anxiety
is not free.

it has cost me
more than i know

how to give.

these days
it's the most

expensive thing
i own.

i can still hear it
in the quiet moments.

i can still hear you
say that you can't go on

loving me.

that there are too many
pieces to carry

and these edges
are too sharp to hold.

we tried
to count the stars
above our heads

and i wondered
how anyone
could see

so much light
and still refer to it
as darkness.

i guess i knew
what tasting your skin
would cost me,

and maybe
that's what love
really is:

standing still
while every sinew
is screaming at you

to run.

i came
into this world

with saltwater
on my lips

and a tongue
forever pressed

against the edges
of goodbye

i have
         given love
    your name
and i still
         can't bring myself
    to say it

sometimes i knock
against the walls of my chest
and hear all the words
i swallowed.

sometimes i just want
to fill it all in,

pack the cavity with soil
and hope
i can remember
how to grow.

THREE

every breath
is a surrender
of life,
of time,

and you made
thousands of mine
worth
           something.

i chisel my name
into every tree i can find,

until blood mingles
with splinters

and blade is indistinguishable
from wood.

i just want
to be remembered;

i just want my name
to be part of something
                    that grows.

she is both
the refuge
and the rocks,
the lighthouse
and the sea.

[She wasn't perfect. She didn't read Ada Limon or Plato. She couldn't play an instrument or talk to me about psychology. She could be petty, jealous; she was often quick to anger. She grew up knowing a kind of trauma I couldn't begin to understand, and her monsters terrified mine. She was insecure, and she could be intensely self-destructive.

I tell you these things because it's important that I remember the person she really was, and so you know that I'm not romanticizing her memory. Because she was also the most beautiful person I have known. She smiled and I would forget everything that had ever drawn my blood; life was easy because she was next to me. She was kind, considerate, selfless and extremely loyal. She was a good friend, a good partner. She was the light when I knew nothing but darkness, and even when loving me meant giving more than she could afford to lose, she kept trying to give. She made me feel at home when I was lost, and safe when the wolves in my chest would stalk me. I am no better off without her than my lungs are without breath.

She has been both my drowning and my shore, the lighthouse and the sea.]

and again
my mind
runs to you
in the way
that rivers
can't help
but return
to the salt

the winter grips
like a dying son
and i realize another year
has passed.

outside, the rain
applauds my loneliness,
my sunken fear
of leaving.

we try not to think
of the past we carry,
slipped beneath
our skin

and sealed tight
with bruises.
but still it finds us, both.
still it demands to be

remembered.

the problem
is this grief
needs more room
than i can give it.

it is such
a wanting, grasping thing,
blood-kissed hands
empty, open.

but nothing here
can be given.
       nothing i have
       is enough.

HOLD MY
HEART
AND WATCH
IT BURN

I PROMISE
YOU CAN KEEP
WHAT THE FIRES
DON'T TAKE

THE WORDS

BREAK DOWN

BEHIND

MY

TEETH

AND BUILD

THEMSELVES

INTO

SOMETHING

DIFFERENT,

SOMETHING

THAT

LOOKS

LIKE

YOU.

i'm sorry. i can't tell you
how to fix a broken heart.

but i can tell you
the importance

of keeping moving.
i can tell you that even

when you have no idea
which direction to go,

bravery is putting one foot
in front of the other anyway.

live with it
long enough
and pain begins
to feel familiar,

even comforting.

when it's
the only constant,
even heartbreak
can find a way

to feel like home.

you rest
the weight of your bones
        on mine

and i can feel
the scars burn
        across my skin,

every one
a metaphor
        for *almost*.

i think they remember
the rough of an edge.
        i think they recognize

those things that cut.

time doesn't work
like it used to:

there is only before, and after.

you introduced yourself
in the same way
a gunshot introduces itself

to the quietest part of the night.

that is to say,
you were all at once.

it writes to me—
           the trauma, i mean.
just postcards, mostly.

cheap prints
with a handwritten note
that usually says,

i remember you.
and i know
           you remember me too.

[Some of the hardest periods of trying to cope with a mind that likes to fold in on itself are the times when you think you're getting better. The wolf steps back into the darkness and you allow yourself to wonder if you've beaten it, if you're no longer a hunted thing. These periods are tough because they make the next panic attack so much harder to deal with. Hope can be a cruel thing.

I've started to think of these relapses into the black as postcards, little messages from the things you've survived. They want you to know that they still remember your name, that the wolf still holds it behind his teeth.]

and her, too.

lost in the wake
of this violent
trembling.

memories
now spindrift:
always evaporating
        (always leaving).

maybe i have
carved through
too many versions
of myself.

maybe i have taken
too much skin,
too much marrow,

and soon the dark
        is all that will remain.

i don't think
i could have loved you
any more than i did.

but i want you
to know, i was prepared
to try.

the rocks at this bottom
are honed,
and their cold
feeds the wanting hollow.

i think i have grown
accustomed to their cutting
and besides,
it's such a long way up

from here.

not everything
broken
can be saved,

because all things can
        be lessened.

break and crush
the glass
into concrete

and eventually it will
        become sand.

and this is how
it took me

(grain
        by grain
  by grain).

EVERYTHING
ABOUT US WAS
A WILDFIRE
AND I STILL
DON'T KNOW IF
WE WERE THE WOOD
OR THE FLAME

the chill bristles across the skin
as we walk, my eyes focused
on you, and yours on your feet.

the silence is telling, now:
each moment an unseized opportunity
for redemption.

even the thunder rolls gently,
the sky apologetically
clearing its throat.

rain falls, cold and soft,
our breath surrendered
to a blinking sky.

i say i'm sorry
and that i love you, and it changes
nothing, means nothing.

i have no metaphors left to wield.
no futures left, other
than those without you.

it's late, and the light
is bruised
     and failing.

i find the usual comfort
in the orange and red
of evening,

in the idea that even
the day is wounded,
     mortal

and falling back
into the darkness.

we built futures
that i'll never get to visit

but i still have to watch
them crumble

i miss you,
by which i mean

i'm jealous
    of the soil
        that gets to hold
            your bones.

i am pulled, still,
to your memory
like the weight of snow
on the youngest branch.

i remember your skin,
        your brittle hands,
and the rhythm of my name
on your voice.

to let these things go
is to grasp at air,
to hold palmfuls of water
in the hope
of conquering thirst.

you left because this
was the only way
you could survive me.

replaced me
on your tongue
with *mistake*

because this
is what i told you
i was.

i didn't mean to be
a close call,
a falling building

you had to drag
yourself
        away from.

i've been writing

        these poems
        looking
        for a way
        to heal

and hoping to god

        i don't
        find one

the phone jolts
and buzzes against
the tiles and suddenly,
i'm here again.

the message is you
just checking i'm okay
and asking if there's
anything i need.

i wonder if
you wouldn't mind
driving the three hundred miles
between us

to pick me up
off the bathroom floor
and remind me
how to breathe.

maybe you could
tidy the apartment?
catch up on the work and,
if it's not too much trouble,

fill the cupboards
with food
and stay long enough
to cook something?

oh, and there's this
pain in my stomach
i still haven't gotten
checked out,

and i keep wanting
to pull the past
from my chest with pliers
(and a lighter).

i message back
to say *i'm fine,*
but thank you
for asking.

please,
just tell me
when this
will end.

how far
do we have
to fall
before gravity

lets us breathe?

collect

enough water

and they will

refer to it as

a body

i don't know
if you are the water
or the light,

only that
you can flood
a room.

[Loving you taught me more than I
ever wanted to learn about loss, and not
nearly enough about belonging. You
showed me how to relearn the word
forgiveness, and pull yearning through
the closing of my throat. But even after
everything we went through, even with
all the words you carved, little more than
ash at my feet, I don't know how to
describe you.

And maybe that's the problem; maybe I
shouldn't be talking about you at all.
Eventually, I'll need to learn to leave the
words behind my tongue, and find a way to
let you go.]

NOT EVERYTHING
THAT GROWS
SHOULD BE
WATERED

behind the clock tower / hands searching /
for themselves / in the darkness /
i touched your skin / to prove that i was still / here /
my breath more than just / a movement of air

SOMEWHERE,
MAYBE YOU AND I

ARE TOGETHER

AND MY THROAT
DOESN'T HOLD

THE DECAYING BONES
OF YOUR NAME

i wonder if the house
mourns us when we leave?

empty, and pining
for the ricochets
of spoken poems
and late-night calls.
there is an empty nest
outside the window

or, there isn't,
but i'm thinking about
the homes
that birds build

and if they miss
the warmth of feathers.

i think not.
my home was once a person
and i don't think
she misses me, either.

before the boards crack
and welcome the hungry sea,
before the last
of these fraying synapses stretch
to another temporary ruin,

let me tell you why we're here.

i've swallowed too many words, love.
too many full stops that grew
into creaking vines.
there are parts of me, now,
that quietly long for wilderness,

that are just too afraid of living.

there is no way this ends
without your hands
wrist-deep in my chest,
and there are too many branches
for you to cut through.

there is too little of me left to love.

she wants me to learn
that grief is borrowed
and must be given back.

i shake my head
and tell her
that this pain was earned.

so keep your medication,
and fold your healing
back behind your tongue.

scratch my name
into the debtors list,
for this sorrow is mine.

i still wear
your goodbye
like a definition.

i guess
i don't know how
to be anything

other
than the person
you left.

it sits with me, across the table,
nails digging into wood.

how are you called? i ask,

and the thing shifts,
teeth grinding violent reds.

i know it won't leave me

even in bruised hours,
in tempest seas,

even with this kerosene-soaked rag
between my molars.

i find pieces of it
under my skin, some days,

amongst the bone shards
and glimmer-blood.

and i wonder if it was here all along.

maybe i grew around it,
and i am the shadow thing.

those hands
are brittle, and held
by skin too quiet
to grasp my leaving.

you can love me,
i swear, but only
after i'm gone,

only once you
recognize that the
difference between
lost and found

is just a question
of timing,
or of seeing,

and that some days
my skin
is the same color
as earth.

i'm not sure
the poetry helps
like it's supposed to,

more self-immolation
than catharsis.

a drowning of sorts,

lungs full
of ink
and water,

all so i might
leave something

behind me.

maybe there's
too much fight
in these hands.

maybe healing
can't be carried
in closed fists.

[It took me a long time to realize that not everything can be approached with closed fists; not every monster can be fought with bare chest and clenched teeth. Some battles must be fought with open hands. Sometimes courage means admitting that you're suffering, letting yourself ask for help.

Sometimes bravery is in the opposite direction to the battlefield.]

the therapist says that
healing is possible,

and somehow
it sounds like

everyone you love
would be better off
without you.

she tells me that
our time is up,

and that sounds
about right.

MURMURATION

Blake Auden is a poet, writer, and artist living in Brighton, UK. Blake has published three previous poetry collections: *Tell the Birds She's Gone, Beekeeper,* and *The Things We Leave Behind.* He is a winner of the Button Poetry 2020 Short Form Prize.

Growing up with a father in the military, Blake began reading war poetry from an early age, becoming fascinated with the ability of prose to capture both deeply traumatic and cathartic experiences. Blake's work now focuses on loss, heartbreak, and mental health.